CW01500758

Contents

MARGARET McALLISTER

Wimmer

Illustrated by
Maureen Bradley

OXFORD
UNIVERSITY PRESS

OXFORD
UNIVERSITY PRESS

Great Clarendon Street, Oxford OX2 6DP

Oxford University Press is a department of the University of Oxford.
It furthers the University's objective of excellence in research, scholarship,
and education by publishing worldwide in

Oxford New York

Athens Auckland Bangkok Bogotá Buenos Aires Calcutta
Cape Town Chennai Dar es Salaam Delhi Florence Hong Kong Istanbul
Karachi Kuala Lumpur Madrid Melbourne Mexico City Mumbai
Nairobi Paris São Paulo Shanghai Singapore Taipei Tokyo Toronto Warsaw

and associated companies in Berlin Ibadan

Oxford is a trade mark of Oxford University Press
in the UK and in certain other countries

British Library Cataloguing in Publication Data
Data available

ISBN 0 19 915968 8

Printed in the UK by Ebenezer Baylis & Son Ltd

Available in packs

Year 6 / Primary 7 Pack of Six (one of each book)   ISBN 0 19 915971 8
Year 6 / Primary 7 Class Pack (six of each book)   ISBN 0 19 915972 6

For Anna Doody of Lady Lumley's School
and for Tom, Stephanie, and all the rest of her
sky-high wonderful English set.

Jacob

1

Finding Him

We found him the way you always find the best things, like sea shells and stones with holes in the middle. By accident.

Mrs Bryant next door had asked me to walk her dog. Mrs Bryant and her dog are both old and a bit creaky, so I often help her, and my sister Polly seems to think I can't walk a dog without her advice. She's like that about most things. So she came, too.

Near our estate there's a wood and fields, but it all belongs to a firm called Newstock Enterprises so it's private land with hedges and barbed wire all round it. Newstock gave the town an adventure playground to make up for us losing the wood, but we couldn't very well walk Suzie in an adventure playground, so we took her along the footpath beside the Newstock hedge. It was September, so there were blackberries and rosehips and things growing along there, tangling round the barbed wire. Polly kept pulling her jacket round her and saying we had to hurry because it was going to rain, but Suzie couldn't hurry if she had to run for her life. She plodded solidly along and sniffed.

"Can't you get a move on?" whinged Polly.

"Go home yourself, if you want to," I said. I had to heave at the lead with both hands because Suzie had stopped to sniff at something in the hedge.

Whatever she'd found, she wasn't going to leave it. Oh, no, not again, I thought. She's a hefty old dog, and if she wants to stay put you can't move her with a JCB. She sat and growled, then the growl changed to a puzzled little whine.

She pricked up her ears lopsidedly, and her gaze was fixed on something under the hedge. I almost expected her to scratch her head, and I got down to see what she'd found.

There he was. He was crouching under the hedge, looking at me from enormous frightened eyes.

I thought at first it was a dog, then a curly-haired cat, then I wasn't sure. It had a wool coat like a poodle's and a strange, bumpy shape to its shoulders, and it was shivering. Its ears looked a size too big for it. They were pointy ears, like a bat's, and they were pressed down flat against its head. It had large dark eyes like a bush-baby's and a cat-like tail, and its colour – well, it was lots of colours running into each other, cream, grey-blue, light brown and a kind of peachy-orange. It looked lost.

I love animals, but we can't have a pet because they give Dad asthma. Mum likes animals too, but she doesn't think they should live in a house. She sometimes lets me look after injured ones in our garden shed. This animal didn't look hurt, but it was terrified.

"Hello," I said to calm it down, "what are you doing there?"

It made a high-pitched sound somewhere between a purr and a growl. You can't rush animals, so I just waited and talked gently to it, like you do, until Polly came rampaging up.

"It'll be pouring in a minute," she said. "What have you found this time?"

I flapped my arm at her to keep quiet but she took no notice, and it had heard her voice. It – he – cowered, his ears flattening more than ever.

"What's this? Oh, somebody's dog," she said, "he must be lost. Has he got a collar?"

"He's terrified," I said. At the sound of my voice his ears lifted again, so I held out both hands and talked to him and he slowly got up. He crouched low to the ground as if he still wasn't sure, but he came. I slipped my hands into the coarse, curly coat and stroked him, and found a plastic collar round his neck.

"Oh, hurry up, Jacob," snapped Polly.

I found his identity tag and held it to the light. 'WIM–R' it said, and beneath, in very small engraving, was a row of letters and figures that looked like a serial number. No name, no address, no telephone number. Just 'WIM–R', whatever that was supposed to mean, and those figures. Seemed odd.

"Its owners will realize it's missing and come for it," said Polly. "It's best to leave it where it is. I'm going. I'll take Suzie."

"I'll be along soon," I said as she dragged Suzie away, and I could feel the creature's tightened muscles relax as I stroked him. His shivering stopped.

"Someone will come for you soon," I said, but nobody came, and the rain pelted harder. It was too far to get him to the police station, and I couldn't take him home.

"They'll come for you," I said once more to the great dark eyes. Then I straightened up and headed home, but I hated that moment, and I hated myself more with every step. I told myself that his owners would come and find him, but what if they didn't? What if he'd been abandoned on purpose? By the time I reached our gate I'd made up my mind to phone the police or the RSPCA or someone,

but as I turned, I noticed something moving
out of the corner of my eye.

He was trotting after me as neatly as can
be, with a trusting look on his face. It was a
look that meant, 'I've found someone who'll
take care of me.'

I knew I shouldn't encourage him. I could
have put him in the shed out of the way, until
I'd reported him to the police, but when I
knelt down he came galloping up, putting his
paws on my knees and stretching up to lick
me. He was my friend. It was in the look on
his face, and the wagging of his skinny tail,
and the touch of his paws on my leg. He liked
me, and I liked him. My friend.

You don't leave your friends
outside in the rain. You
don't shut them
in the garden
shed, either.

Polly

2

Strange Noises

Do you think it's easy, being an older sister? Let me tell you, it's hard work and a lot of responsibility. I don't know what our Jacob would do without me.

He doesn't think, ever. If he takes Suzie for a walk by himself, he'll promise to be back in half an hour. Two hours later he turns up with Suzie covered in burrs and goosegrass and up to her middle in mud. It usually turns out that he's let her off the lead and she's gone chasing rabbits.

She ran on to Newstock land once. If she

wasn't a dog they'd have arrested her for trespass.

That's just Suzie. You never know what he's going to find. We've had lame frogs, birds with broken wings and a very sick hedgehog with fleas. He doesn't bring them into the house, of course. If one paw comes over the doorstep, Dad starts wheezing and Mum has a tantrum. Jacob runs an intensive care unit in the garden shed. Poor Jacob, he never learns. He got bitten rescuing a shrew from a cat. And just don't ask about the hedgehog.

I blame Uncle Colin. He's nice, and the work he does is really good – he works at a wildlife park, but they have an animal sanctuary there too, and we sometimes go there in the holidays. He's Jacob's hero. Jacob wants to do that kind of job when he grows up.

Apart from that, Jacob's almost normal. He draws pictures of helicopters and spaceships, he thinks football is worth ruining a good Saturday for, and he'd wear the same pair of socks every day until they walked off his feet and jumped out of the window. And he'd never do a decent piece of homework if I didn't help him.

The minute he came in that day I knew he'd hidden that animal somewhere, so when lunch was finished and Mum and Dad were out of the way, I watched him go up to his room. Listening outside, I heard whispering and some snuffly noises. I knocked on the door and slipped in.

Jacob glanced up with a cross, guilty face. If he could have hidden the animal he would, but no chance. It was eating little bits of bread and sausage

from his fingers, and looking pleased with itself.

"I never said you could come in," he muttered.

"Bit late now," I said, and shut the door behind me. "Is that from your own lunch?"

He didn't answer, just smiled down at the creature. "He likes it. He's really hungry." When he glanced up at me, his eyes were nearly as appealing as the animal's. "You're not going to tell anyone, are you?"

How could I? The animal turned its head and looked at me from those enormous bush-baby eyes, and wagged its little tail. It was a bonny little thing, in a peculiar way. But it was a bonny little thing in Jacob's bedroom.

When it had licked every last taste of sausage from Jacob's fingers, it lapped up some water from a margarine tub and washed its whiskers with one, neat, peach-coloured paw.

"At least it has clean habits," I said. "More like a cat than a dog. It isn't really a dog, is it?"

"Him, not it," said Jacob. (I hadn't looked, but I took his word for it.) "I'm calling him Wimmer, like it says on his tag."

"Is he house-trained?" I asked.

"He's very clean!" said Jacob indignantly. "He hasn't done anything!"

"All the same, he's not ours, and he can't stay here," I said. "Come on, Jacob. Mum and Dad mustn't know he's been in the house. We'll take him to the police station in town."

Of course, Jacob knew we'd have to do that. He nodded his head, but he kept stroking the odd-looking animal.

"In a minute," he said, in a small, sad voice. "We'll take him in a minute."

The creature put its paw on Jacob's knee, tilted its head and made happy little purring noises at him.

Then it climbed into his lap, licked his face, and cuddled up to him.

Thanks a million, creature, I thought. That really makes it easy to send you away. Jacob's head was bent over him.

"He's tired," he pleaded, and stroked the curly head. "We can't take him now."

"We'll carry him," I said firmly. "That way, we won't need a lead." Just as well, because we didn't have one.

"He wouldn't run off, anyway." Jacob smiled down as it twitched its ears. "He's really good."

It purred again, but this time we both stared at it, then at each other. It had purred a tune.

Not exactly a tune, but it had picked up the sound of Jacob's last sentence, the way his voice went up and down. Try closing your mouth and humming, 'he's really good'. That's the way he purred.

"He didn't really do that," I said quickly, but Jacob said it again. "He's really good." The creature copied him again.

"It's a coincidence," I said.

"No it isn't, he meant it!" said Jacob. "He's copying speech! I told him he was really good, loads of times, before you came in, and he's learned it. Watch. Wimmer, look at me." It did. "You're really good."

"Mm-mm-m-mm," it purred again. It spooked me.

"It may not be exactly a dog, but it's not a parrot, either," I said. "Now we've got to get it moved, sharpish. I'll pay your bus fare."

I told Mum and Dad we were going into town, which was true, and we went out with the creature trotting at Jacob's heel. It was amazingly obedient. Along the garden wall there's a fence and a flowerbed with pansies and things in it, which is where Wimmer sniffed a bit, then decided to dig.

"No!" said Jacob, but it was too late. Wimmer had his head down over the hole and probably couldn't hear a thing, and you should have seen him dig! Left alone much longer, he could have been half-way to Australia. The paws scrabbled, the earth flew

up, his head disappeared lower and lower –
then just when I thought he'd fall in, he
stopped, turned round, and, with his head
down and his eyes tight shut, shook the loose
soil out of his ears. Then a glazed expression
came over his face. He settled himself over the
hole, lifted his tail, and – er – oh, you know
what he did.

You can't hurry nature, but I was desperate
to get him away from there. What if Mum
looked out, or somebody arrived and saw
him? We couldn't stop him, once he'd started.
I stood in front of him, Jacob stood behind
him, and we both tried to look innocent.

Strangely, there was no smell. When
Wimmer had finished he scrabbled the earth
neatly back in again. I wouldn't have been
surprised if he'd planted a pansy on the top.

The bus stop was outside the main gates of
Newstock, and I was hoping we wouldn't
meet anyone we knew on the way. We were all
right, with Wimmer trotting beside Jacob,
until we crossed the road.

We got to the other side and Wimmer

stopped as if he'd slammed the brakes on. His ears flattened against his head and he cowered back, with a little high-pitched growl like a food mixer. Then, just when I thought we'd

have to pick him up and carry him he sprang forward and shot into the hedge with our Jacob after him. I could hear whimpery noises from Wimmer and Jacob trying to calm him down, but I couldn't see a thing.

I wasn't going to crawl about in a hedge, so I stood and waited for them. We were near the bus stop, and I wanted to keep a lookout in case the bus arrived. So there I was, looking along the road, when this long, shiny, grey car came swishing up the Newstock drive. The automatic gate lifted for it, and I stood back so it couldn't swoosh through the puddles and splash me, but it slowed and stopped. A window glided down.

In the passenger seat was a tall man with short, curly blond hair and a long narrow face. He looked as if he was gazing just over the top of my head and thinking of something more important. At the wheel sat a woman with neat short hair, dark and very glossy, and a stern expression. She looked as if she should be a guard at a high security prison. She turned off the engine, got out without speaking and crossed the road, where she seemed to be looking for something. The man spoke to me.

"We're looking for our dog," he said in a long, lazy kind of way as if he had all the time in the world. "You haven't seen a stray dog, have you? Small, greyish, pointy ears. Funny-looking thing."

It wasn't the only thing that looked funny to me. Not just funny. Fishy.

You might think I didn't care about

Wimmer as much as Jacob did. You may be right. But I wasn't going to say, 'yes, I've seen your dog, as you call him, and he's hiding in that hedge because this place scares him out of his wits'. He hadn't come running to meet them, had he?

"I haven't..." I began, then I thought again. "Yes, I think I might have seen him," I said loudly, so Jacob would hear. "He had big eyes. He was running about on the main road – look, I'll show you. That way."

I pointed in the opposite direction from the hedge where Jacob and Wimmer were hidden, then I sort of gabbled. I don't know what I said, something about dogs running off, and weren't the roads dangerous – anything to cover up the rustlings in the hedge. I was dying to look round and make sure they were well hidden. One trainer sticking out would have ruined everything, but I didn't dare look.

"On the Staveley Road, heading for the by-pass," I said. "I was afraid he might get run over. What do you call him?"

"Call him?" For a moment he looked like

a kid who's been caught daydreaming in class, then he pulled himself together. "Er – Ben," he said. He must have taken me for an idiot.

"In the car," snapped the woman. I thought she meant me, but she was talking to the man. When she grumbled something about "stupid thing", she still might have meant me, but I think she was talking about the animal. He took a business card from his pocket and gave it to me.

"Thanks ever so much," he drawled. "If you see it again, would you be the most absolute poppet and give me a buzz? The mobile number is on there, and the e-mail, and the fax. I'm Dr Hugh Harper of Newstock Enterprises. Or you could ask for my colleague here, Dr Sheridan. Nice to meet you." He still sounded vague and laid back, but Dr Sheridan started the car and they roared off like the Grand Prix.

I still didn't dare look towards the hedge until they were out of sight and couldn't see me in the mirror. Then a muffled voice said,

"Have they gone?"

Jacob scrambled out with bits of leaf and twig all over him, scratches on his hands, and Wimmer huddling against him in his arms. As Jacob stroked him the trembling stopped and the ears lifted, one at a time.

"We can't take him to the police now," he said. "They'd give him back to those people." And I knew he was right.

Jacob

3

Now What?

Wimmer lay quietly in my arms when the man and woman had gone.

I was curious about Newstock. Nobody seemed to know what went on there. It was something to do with services to farms, but they never explained exactly what they did. With the hedges and the barbed wire, you'd think it was a nuclear weapons plant. My friend's mum had worked there and left, and never talked about it, but she wasn't happy about Newstock.

No way was Wimmer going back. We

brought him home. Even Polly could see it was for the best.

It was just my luck that Dad was in the hall when we got back. Dad, by the way, is tall and hefty and he's an engineer. (I'm not sure what sort of engines.) Mum's little and round and she's a health visitor. Think of a bottle and a jug, that's what Mum and Dad look like.

Luckily, Polly got in first. I slipped round the corner of the house where I couldn't be seen, picked up Wimmer and zipped my jacket round him. Polly kept Dad talking.

"The bus didn't come," she said, "so we're not going to town today."

"Aren't you coming in, Jacob?" yelled Dad from the doorway.

"Yes," I said, but Wimmer poked his head out and had a look round. "In a minute," I added, and pushed him back, but he stuck out a paw. I gave up, took the jacket off and wrapped him up in it like fish and chips in paper.

"Why aren't you wearing your jacket?" asked Dad, like I knew he would.

"Didn't need it on," I said, and nipped up the stairs.

What's that?" said Dad.

Oh, no, just leave me alone, I thought. Just go away!

"What's what?" I said, and tried to look clueless. Polly was running up the stairs behind me.

"That," said Dad. I looked down. Wimmer's tail was hanging out under my arm.

"It's the tie thing off his jacket," said Polly, and tucked it in. "I've told you about that, Jacob."

"Looks a bit funny to me," said Dad.

"Dad," said Polly patiently, "it's called a tail tie. Everyone wears them."

I don't know how she gets away with it. He believed her. He always does. We got Wimmer up to my bedroom and put him on the floor, where he rolled over to have his tummy tickled.

"Now what?" said Polly. "We can't take him back and we can't keep him." Wimmer purred and licked me.

"We have to keep him," I said, "just for the moment." I wanted that moment to be forever. Sooner or later, I'd have to part with him, and I didn't want to think about that. He was the best thing in the world to me.

I reckoned the RSPCA might find him a home. But we had to hide him until the Newstock people had stopped looking for him.

Thinking of them, I felt as if a shadow had come across the sun. Why did he tremble and hide when they were near? Nobody would hurt him, would they? He must have wondered why I'd stopped fussing him, because he sat up and put a paw on my knee. I stroked him, and felt the bumps behind his shoulders.

"Those bumps are getting bigger," I said, "feel."

"You're imagining it," said Polly. "Now, if you're going to keep him he has to be fed, exercised, and kept out of the way. Have you got that?" Honestly, she should be in the army.

We worked out a plan. We'd feed him on leftovers and stuff, and buy dog food and things at the corner shop. I wanted him to live in my bedroom, but on schooldays we'd have to put him in the shed in case Mum came in.

Exercise looked like a big problem. We couldn't take him round the park without people noticing him. If word got back to Harper and Sheridan he'd be in danger, and if it got back to Mum and Dad, we'd be in deep trouble. Polly had a bright idea. She had a paper round first thing in the morning, and it's very quiet then. We decided that she'd wake me early when she was doing her round, and I'd take him to the park. In the meantime, it was a case of nipping into the back garden with him when the parents weren't likely to be looking. We wished we could make it safer, though.

"Could we dye him a different colour?" said Polly.

"That's cruel. No," I said.

"Put him in a coat or something?"

"So's that. No."

"Creep out in the middle of the night to walk him?"

"No," I said.

"Oh?" said Wimmer.

He didn't exactly say it, but that's what it sounded like. It was scary, in a way.

"Oh," he said again, or rather, barked.

"He did that before, remember?" I said. "He copies speech, like a parrot." I wanted to teach him 'Jacob', but Polly interrupted, as usual.

"If he's that clever, has he learned to obey commands?" She stood up, with her back to the door. "Wimmer, come!"

He trotted up to her like a show dog and she did all that 'sit, stay,' stuff that you do to train a dog. He must have already learned it, because he did everything right.

"He's brilliant," I said. "I bet he could open the door if he wanted to."

He must have learned the phrase 'open the door' from somebody at Newstock. He trotted to the door and looked at it with his head on one side. He stood on his hind legs and pushed, but that didn't work, so he tried curling one paw round it, like a cat. That was no good, either, so I opened it for him, and shut it again.

"No!" said Polly.

"Oh!" said Wimmer again, wagging his tail. He put up one paw, pressed the handle, opened the door, then ran up to me to be fussed, tail going like a banner and very proud of himself.

"That was clever," said Polly in her headmistress voice. "Now how are you going to keep him in?" I hadn't thought of that.

She was worried that he'd open the door and follow us downstairs at teatime, but I told him to stay. When I went back upstairs he hadn't moved from the spot, gazing at the door with big, brown eyes and scampering up to me as soon as I walked in. The bumps on his back seemed bigger than ever, but I was more interested in feeding him. I'd brought him some jacket potato skins, vegetables, and a biscuit, and he ate it all.

You know how it is on Christmas Eve, when you really want to hurry up and go to bed? It was like that. I wanted it to be night. I wanted it to be late enough to go to bed, so I'd have my pet - well, he was almost my pet -

sleeping in my bedroom. I'd made him a nest with a couple of old sweaters and stuff. He scraped it about, settled down, and licked me. He was still telling me – you're my friend. We took off his collar because he didn't seem to belong to us with that on. Polly said I'd only lose it, so she put it away safely.

When I did go to bed I left the light on for ages so I could watch him. He lay curled up

tightly with one peach-coloured paw over his nose, while I watched the up and down of his breathing. I fell asleep thinking that Wimmer and I were breathing each other's breath.

It was still grey outside when a damp

snuffling woke me up. Before I opened my eyes I reached out to stroke Wimmer's curly head. Then I woke up properly, and saw his two front paws on the bed, so I lifted him on to the duvet. He turned round, sighed happily, and fell asleep again, and I sat up to look at the bumps on his back.

They weren't bigger. But they'd grown feathers. Blue-grey feathers.

Polly

4

Polly's Choice

For Jacob, it was just an animal that needed him. It could have had three tails and purple polka dots, he wouldn't have cared. But I kept getting that collar out and wishing it would tell us something more. Why WIM? Why the dash before the 'R'? Why the serial number?

Jacob thought he was beautiful. Some people would have said he was ugly. To me, he was cute in a peculiar sort of way, and he had a lovely nature, but he was never a normal dog, even when we first found him.

Believe me, when you see a dog with

feathers you think you've been out in the sun too long. When Jacob woke me up at some appalling hour in the morning and showed me those feathers, I wanted it to be a bad dream, but it wasn't. It made me wonder what exactly they were up to at Newstock.

I'd got it into Jacob's head that Wimmer would have to stay in the shed on schooldays. If Mum had gone into Jacob's bedroom and found him she'd still be stuck to the ceiling when we got back. Jacob didn't like it, but he could see it made sense.

We managed to keep Wimmer quiet on Sunday. He seemed to know what was wanted, and apart from those funny noises as if he was trying to speak, he didn't bark, even when the doorbell rang. Jacob taught him to hide under the bed and stay there if anybody came past the door, so I hoped he'd have the sense to hide under the wheelbarrow if anybody went in the shed. It would freak Mum out if she decided to sweep up some leaves and found a pair of bat ears sticking out of a flowerpot. Sitting in Jacob's bedroom on Sunday night, I seemed to find one problem after another.

"What if he forgets to stay put?" I said. "What if he hears Mum coming and thinks it's you, and gets out? What if he needs a wee?" Half past eight in the morning to half past three in the afternoon was a long time for him to wait.

"He's perfectly clean, aren't you, Wimmer?" said Jacob, but it still seemed risky to me. I wished I could talk to Uncle Colin and ask his advice, but I couldn't. We were keeping an animal that rightly belonged to Newstock, and we had no intention of letting them take him back. We couldn't involve anybody else unless it became a matter of life or death.

* * *

First thing on Monday morning we smuggled Wimmer into the shed with his bedding and an old cuddly toy that Jacob had given him. I don't know if Jacob concentrated on any work that day, but I certainly didn't. How I

got away without a detention is a miracle.
Jacob finishes before I do, so he's always
home first. I got back as soon as I could,
dumped my bag and my coat, and went to
the shed.

I knew something was wrong before I
opened the door. It felt too quiet. Jacob was
sitting hunched up with his back to me and his
head down, and Wimmer in his arms.

He heard me come in, but he didn't say
anything. He just got to his feet and turned
round, and I've never, ever, seen such misery.
His eyes were so pink and swimmy I don't
think he could see properly, and his whole
face was wet and swollen. He
lifted Wimmer towards me.
Limp, cold Wimmer.
His eyes were shut.

I snatched him out of Jacob's arms and Jacob grabbed to get him back, but I held on. Wimmer mustn't be dead. It mustn't happen.

He was cool, but not stiff – that was something. I put him on the floor and felt for a pulse, but I didn't know where to look for a pulse in an animal. I tried behind his ear.

Nothing.

He couldn't die. Jacob loved him too much. He'd been fine in the morning. I felt his paws and under his chin, but I still couldn't find a pulse amongst all that fur.

Trying to ignore the sniffs and gulps from Jacob, I told myself to think. If there was anything normal about Wimmer, he'd at least have his heart in his chest somewhere. I turned him over and put my fingers on his ribs.

I felt a faint touch of movement, very slow. After each flutter of pulse there was a long pause before the next, but his heart was still beating.

I thought of Uncle Colin again, and how I'd decided we mustn't involve him except in a case of life or death. I bundled Wimmer back

into Jacob's arms.

"He's alive, but only just," I said. "Rub his paws. Talk to him."

He wiped his face with his hand and took Wimmer's paw. "Where are you going?" he asked.

"To phone Uncle Colin."

He didn't seem to have heard. "Just a minute," he said, not looking at me.

"What now?" I snapped. It was his pet I was trying to save, for heaven's sake!

"He's looking at me!"

I spun round. Wimmer's eyes were open, and he was gazing at Jacob's face. Then he licked him, wriggled, jumped down and put his paws up to be fussed, bouncing around like any normal dog.

Wimmer's heart might be all right, but mine was doing somersaults. The wretched thing had me worried sick, then a minute later he's leaping about like a box of frogs.

"Two-faced little mongrel," I said, but I was so glad he was all right, I could forgive him for scaring us half to death. Jacob was hugging him, rolling him over and tickling his tummy, but he had to be practical.

"Check his food and water," I said, and of course Jacob said he was just going to. In fact, Wimmer had hardly touched what we'd left for him in the morning, but now he had a long drink of water and ate everything in his bowl.

"Now take him outside, so he can..."

"I was JUST GOING TO!" insisted Jacob, but he had to say that. We took Wimmer outside and kept an eye on the house while he did what he had to do. It wasn't a good time to take him for a walk, but we let him have a run about in the garden. He chased after leaves and pounced on them the way a kitten does, but with little snuffly growls, and his smooth, skinny tail swished from side to side. He looked almost normal, except for his feathers. I tried to ignore them.

If you try really hard, you can ignore the fact that a dog has feathers. You have to be determined, but you can do it. What you can't ignore is a dog spreading its wings, and that's what he did.

He stopped chasing a leaf, rolled over, and wriggled his nose against his back as if he had an itch. Then he rolled over again and did the same on the other side. It made us laugh, then he stood up as if he'd suddenly decided to be dignified. He sneezed. Then he spread his wings.

They weren't very big wings, but they were thick and strong, and multi-coloured like the rest of him. He stretched and closed them as if he was trying them out, and twisted his neck to try and get a good look at them. I think he was even more surprised than we were.

"Magic!" whispered Jacob.

"Weird," I said. What would he do next? Grow wheels and an engine?

There was no time to think about it, not with Wimmer scampering about the lawn and trying out his wings. He took a short run, rose from the ground, flew for about a metre at knee height, and landed at Jacob's feet.

"Well done, flying ace!" yelled Jacob.

"Shut up!" I glanced over my shoulder at the house. "Don't encourage him. How can we control him if he can fly away?"

"He can't fly much," said Jacob, but Wimmer was still learning. He flew a bit further and a bit higher next time, and the time after that he was nearly up to Jacob's shoulder, with Jacob cheering him on and telling him how clever he was. He was wheeling round lopsided like an aeroplane, higher and higher, above Jacob's head. I don't know what he would have done, if he hadn't flown into a tree.

One minute he was whizzing about like a frisbee, and the next his little hind paws had disappeared into the top branches. There was

a sharp "orraworrawoop" from somewhere among the leaves.

Jacob was ready to skim up after him and get him out, but I stopped him. "Wait," I said. "See if he can get down by himself."

There was a bit of rustling and scuffling, and we could see the tips of two ears sticking up through the leaves. Then it rustled a bit more and his tail appeared, but he must have realized he was back to front because the tail vanished, the leaves shook, and he peeped through the leaves like a little gnome. The branches wobbled under him, and he whimpered a bit.

"Go on, then," I said to Jacob, but he was already up the tree. I knew that if Wimmer was going to make a habit of getting stuck up trees he'd have to learn to get out of them, but no way was our kid going to leave him there. Fortunately Jacob was better at getting up trees than Wimmer was at getting down them. He'd just about reached him when Mum came to call us for tea.

That was when Wimmer looked out. It was only a second, the second before Jacob got to him and pulled him back out of sight, but I could tell from the puzzled look on Mum's face that she'd seen something in that tree that didn't belong there. I had to distract her.

"I'm starving, what's for tea!" I said brightly, determined to say 'fantastic!' even if it was shepherd's pie and turnip. But Mum was looking at the tree.

"There's something in the beech tree," she said. "I saw a funny face."

"It's Jacob," I said loudly, and Jacob looked out with a stupid grin.

"Not Jacob," she insisted. "I wonder if we've got a squirrel?"

"Wouldn't that be great, Mum!" I said.

"Well, get out of that tree, Jacob, before you frighten it away," she said, and frowned. There was a loud rustle and a cry of "oops, ouch!" from Jacob and a muffled bark from Wimmer.

"What's for tea, then?" I said again. I had to say it loudly, in case Wimmer made any noise that couldn't come from Jacob or a squirrel.

"Shepherd's pie and turnip," she said.

Well, at least Wimmer could have mine. He was happy to eat anything, he wasn't fussy. We fed him my shepherd's pie after tea, and I left Jacob playing with him while I went to the corner shop.

I thought it might look conspicuous if we kept buying dog food, so I bought him some biscuits instead. I was paying for them when I had an idea.

There are always adverts in the shop-window, mostly 'for sale' and 'wanted', but sometimes people advertise for missing pets. I took a look. One black cat had been reported missing, and that was all. I asked the woman at the counter if anybody had come in to ask about a small, lost dog, but she said no, nobody at all.

When somebody's lost a much-loved pet, they put it in every shop-window, tie posters around lamp-posts and ask around the houses. Dr Harper and Dr Sheridan didn't seem to be making any effort to find him. That was a bit strange, when I thought about it. It was almost as if they didn't want anyone to know about him.

From the phone box, I rang the RSPCA and the police. They said nobody had enquired about a strange-looking dog with big eyes and bat ears. (I didn't mention the wings.)

I still had Dr Harper's card in my pocket. I decided there were things I needed to know, and only one way to find out. There was something secretive and a bit scary about Newstock and about Dr Harper, too, but I had to phone him. And I had to do it immediately, before I had time to talk myself out of it.

He answered the phone, and I took a deep breath. "My name's Katie Hunter," I lied. "I met you outside Newstock the other day, when you were looking for your dog. Is it still missing? I think I may have seen it on Chad's Hill." (That was miles away, so it would keep him off the scent.) "Can you tell me a bit more about him?"

That slow, lazy voice purred back over the phone to me. "That really is very helpful of you, Katie. It would be best if you could come and see me. Can you come here, to Newstock, say, tomorrow? After school?"

I didn't want to go in there, but it was a chance to learn something about Wimmer. So, by the time I left the phone box, I had an appointment to go and see Dr Harper. I also had a simple terror of walking into the Newstock building and hearing the door shut behind me.

The scariest thing was this – I'd have to do it on my own. I couldn't even tell Jacob, because he'd make a fuss about wanting to come too.

I didn't like putting myself in danger. I certainly couldn't do it to Jacob.

Jacob

5

The Hunt Begins

Polly said at breakfast that she'd be late home from school. She said she had to practise for something, and as Polly thinks that the choir and the drama group can't manage without her, I didn't take much notice. I was still thinking about Wimmer.

I thought about him all day at school, and when I got home Mum made the usual fuss about my games kit: "You must have been mud wrestling! Put it in the wash this minute!" I'd left my trainers at school, but it was safest not to tell her that. She'd send me all the way back for them. I only wanted to be with Wimmer, and soon I was in the shed.

He was in that deep sleep again, but this time I wasn't worried. I talked to him and felt for his heartbeat the way I'd seen Polly do it, and he wriggled and came to life, twitching his ears and shaking his wings.

There was nobody watching. If Mum's home at that time of day, she's usually cooking and the kitchen doesn't look over the garden, and Dad doesn't get home till late. I let Wimmer out. He'd found an old tennis ball in the shed, so we played with that.

It was fun, but in our garden I couldn't throw it very far. Wimmer could see which way I aimed the throw and get there before the ball did, so I had to pretend to throw it and then chuck it the other way when he wasn't looking. He soon got wise to that.

I tried throwing it in the air, and he jumped for it. I threw it a bit higher, and he flew. I threw it higher again, so he had to fly higher and further.

He was having such a great time that I

forgot to be careful. I kept
throwing the ball and Wimmer kept flying to
catch it, and then it landed in a tree. So did

Wimmer, when he went after it.

It wasn't our tree. It was Mrs Bryant's, next door, and I'd seen what Wimmer was like with trees.

It was near enough to our beech tree to climb up and try to get him out from there, so I scrambled up, talking to him all the way, telling him to keep still, and not to panic. I was in such a hurry I got clumsy and slipped a few times, but I got there at last.

"Wimmer," I said, "It's OK! I'm here!"

I was there, but he wasn't. I saw empty branches where he'd been. I looked all round, and I still couldn't see him anywhere.

I jumped down, dashed next door and told Mrs Bryant that I'd lost my ball, and she let me go and look for it. I went crawling under bushes and hunting in the flowerbeds, whispering Wimmer's name.

Not even a feather. I guessed he must have panicked and flown away, and lost his sense of direction. I tried the houses on either side. No good.

I didn't know how long he could keep

flying, and neither did he. He could be in the next street, or miles away.

Sooner or later, somebody would find him. It could be somebody like me and Polly, who'd take care of him, or it could be the Newstock people, or worse. I had to get to him before anybody else did.

There's a hill near us called Lookout Hill because of the view from the top. There was just a chance I could see him if I climbed up there. I kept scanning the hedges as I went past, because that was how I'd found him in the first place, hiding in a hedge. Then the rain began and I wished I'd brought my jacket, but I couldn't waste time going back for it.

Wimmer was lost, and he must be frightened. He might think I'd given up on him. Just thinking of that hurt me, really hurt. Still keeping an eye on the hedges, glancing up at the sky in case he was flying, I ran for Lookout Hill.

Polly

6

The Newstock Files

It's lonely being a heroine.

I'm not saying I was a heroine. I was just doing what I had to do for Wimmer and Jacob, and anybody would do the same. I was curious – I wanted to know what was going on at Newstock – but I was terrified too.

I couldn't ask anyone's advice or help. There was just me, in my school uniform with a bit of mascara and stuff to make me look older and more confident. I even varnished my nails. I had ink on my fingers and it wouldn't wash off. I was hoping nobody would notice it.

So that was me, strolling into the Newstock offices when all the time I wanted to turn around and run the other way. I told the receptionist that I was Katie Hunter and I had an appointment with Dr Harper, and she pressed a button so that the doors glided open for me. They glided shut behind me, too, and gave me a cold feeling down my spine. Dr Harper's secretary led me to another office, checked the desk diary, and picked up a phone.

There was a door leading to Dr Harper's room, but she couldn't just knock and tell him I was there, could she? She had to speak to him on the phone. Then, at last he appeared, looking taller than ever in that small space, with a smile that was a bit too charming.

"How lovely to see you, Katie," he said, and shook my hand. "Excuse me for one moment." He looked past me to the secretary. "Lisa, I hope you remembered that those letters must be in tonight's post," he said sharply. "And I want the figures on poultry food by ten o'clock tomorrow." She pulled a

face as if she'd
just bitten a
lemon, but he
didn't take any notice.

He was leading me into his office by then. If
you want to know what that felt like, think of
being at the dentist.

It was a very small, neat room. Too neat, as
if it had just been tidied. Dr Harper indicated
a chair for me then sat down, folded his
hands, and raised an eyebrow.

"What did you want to talk to me about,
Katie?" he asked in his slow, smooth way.

"Take as long as you like, there's plenty of time."

"I wondered if there was any news of your dog," I said.

"Yes," he drawled. "We went to Chad's Hill, and I did catch sight of him." (Lie number one, I thought.) "Unfortunately, that was all. Have you seen him again?"

"No, but I'll help look for him," I said. "I've forgotten his name."

"Oh, we call him Tim, but it's not important," he said. "There's no need to worry. I'm sure he'll turn up."

Lie number two. He was 'Ben' on Saturday. I'd seen Dr Harper's eyes flicker across the desk, and I think he got the name 'Tim' from a letter that was lying there. He might as well have said the dog was called telephone. "The police would help," I suggested. "Is he micro-chipped?"

He smiled again, but with more difficulty this time. I was becoming a nuisance. "He will have arrived on Dr Sheridan's doorstep by now, I'm sure. It's very sweet of you to be so concerned about him, my dear, but you shouldn't worry."

I could see that any minute now he was going to phone through to his secretary and ask her to show me out. I couldn't let that happen. I hadn't discovered anything yet.

"If you would give me a description, it would help," I said, but he reached for the phone. I wanted to scream, 'It's WIM!', but it wouldn't have helped a lot.

If I let on that I knew anything about Wimmer, Harper would never let me go. Not until I'd told him everything.

"Show Katie out, please, Lisa," he said down the telephone. I blurted out the first thing I could think of.

"Is there something the matter with his back?"

It worked. The secretary came to the door, and Dr Harper gave her his lazy smile and sent her away. But he wasn't smiling at me, not after she shut the door. I crossed my fingers and sat on my hand.

"Please explain," he said. "What's this

about his back?"

"It's bumpy," I said.
"Has he ever been
injured?" I was sitting
on both hands now, so he
wouldn't see them shaking.

"He's a rare breed," he said, but he
sounded ruffled. "Do tell me more. Apart
from that, did he look all right?"

He wanted to find out how much I knew,
but he'd just given me the chance to question
him about this rare breed of dog. I was about
to ask where they got him from, when the
phone rang.

"Hello? Denise!" he said. His face lit up with sharp excitement and he waved his hand to shoo me out into the secretary's office. He lowered his voice, but by dawdling near the door I could still hear him saying something about "where?" and "sure?" and then, "in a minute". Presently he came out with his coat over his arm and his briefcase in his hand.

"I'm afraid I have to go now, so Lisa will show you out," he said as he strode past me, then he seemed to change his mind. "On second thoughts, please wait in my office. There's coffee in the machine, help yourself. I won't be long."

I'd worked out exactly what was happening. Denise was Dr Sheridan, and she'd seen Wimmer. At least, she thought she had. She must have been mistaken, because Wimmer was still in our shed. And Dr Harper wanted to keep me there until he'd found out exactly how much I knew.

A sensible voice inside me told me to get out, sharpish. Another voice said I should find out all I could while he was out of the way.

The door to the secretary's office was open and it would have looked suspicious if I'd shut it, so I couldn't search his room. There were letters on the desk, but he'd taken care not to leave anything important where I might see it. A computer stood on a separate table, but I reckoned it would be protected with a password. The only other thing I could see was a cupboard marked 'Cleaning Materials Only', and I couldn't imagine him keeping top secret files in there with the bleach and the hoover. I drank coffee and tried not to nibble my nails because the varnish comes off if you do that.

I was just wondering if I should create a diversion by saying I was going to be sick, when the receptionist arrived to talk to the secretary. "Simon's just got his holiday photographs back," she said. "Want to come and see?" They glanced at me, and I tried to look bored.

"Why not?" said Lisa. "Grumpyguts is out, and the kid's just here for a school project or something, aren't you?"

I nodded and hoped I looked suitably thick. When the two of them went off together, I moved fast. I tried all the desk drawers, but they were locked.

The secretary might have a set of keys. Normally I wouldn't dream of doing anything like this and I felt like a thief, but I had to. I hunted right through her desk – not a key in sight. There was a scrap of paper with a number on it, and I looked at it, memorized it, and put it back. It was 5612.

It might have been a cash card number or something, one of those that you're not supposed to write down. But I remembered it, just in case it was a security code for a lock.

I went back into Dr Harper's office. All his desk drawers opened with a key, so I was no further on. The only thing in the office with one of those locks where you have to tap in a security code was the cleaning cupboard, and...

Hang on, I thought. Why do you need a coded lock on the cleaning cupboard?

I dashed to the door, and pressed 5612 on

the lock. Nothing happened. I did it again in case I'd got it wrong. Nothing again. Maybe she'd deliberately written it down back to front or inside out. I tried every combination of 5612 I could think of. I don't know which one of them worked in the end, but something did, and I was in.

There were cleaning materials in there, just as it said. There were boxes of bleach and washing-up liquid, and cans of polish. There was also some kind of box, a laptop computer, and a briefcase.

I expected that to be locked, too, but it wasn't. I unzipped it, and found four neat folders inside. I drew them out one by one, not even sure what I was looking for. The first three were full of figures and formulas that made no sense to me at all, and the last was grey and very thin, as if it was trying not to be there at all.

Something about it caught my eye. I saw the tiny letters in the top right hand corner, so small and neat that I only noticed them, because they were already in my heart and mind all the time. WIM.

Outside, there was a shriek of laughter and I heard people talking. I hugged the folder tight, pressed myself into the darkest corner of the cupboard, and tried to think of something to say if anyone found me in there.

How could I explain why I was in the broom cupboard? Easy. I couldn't. And I mustn't be found with that file in my arms. Shaking so much I nearly dropped it, I shoved it under the lid of that box thing. Then I saw that it wasn't a box at all. It was a photocopier.

I stayed still, shaking and feeling a bit sick, while outside they went on chatting. I thought they'd be there for ever. Finally, somebody said, "Where's that school kid?"

"Gone, I suppose. Tired of waiting for Grumpyguts. Who cares?" They laughed again, and their voices faded into the distance.

I was still shaking, but I managed to whisk the papers out of the file and press the right buttons on the photocopier. I was afraid it might make a noise, but it was completely silent. It was as if it was meant for secrecy.

Jacob

7

Closing In

Polly's a pain sometimes, but as I ran up Lookout Hill I was wishing she was there to help. Every minute Wimmer was out on his own, he was in danger.

Cold rain seeped through my hair onto my scalp and trickled down my neck. Soon, it was sticking my trousers to my legs and squelching in my shoes, and after that, I didn't care any more. This was for Wimmer. Standing at the top of Lookout Hill, I bawled his name.

I turned round slowly. There was the river at the bottom of the hill behind me with fields on the other side, then the by-pass. In front and to the right were our estate, my school, and the town, and on the left was Newstock. He wouldn't go there.

I was soaking wet and looking for a small, frightened animal in the pouring rain. Hopeless. Everybody who'd ever said I was an idiot must be right. I could see cars sloshing through the puddles, and rain bouncing off the school tennis courts.

Then I saw something. It wasn't Wimmer. It made me feel even colder than I was already.

It was that car, the one from Newstock. I'd seen it on the Saturday, when I was hiding in the hedge with Wimmer. It was moving very, very, slowly, creeping round those streets like a cat stalking round a bird table.

I could think of only one reason why anyone would be driving it like that. They were looking for something. Almost certainly Wimmer. Somebody from Newstock must have caught sight of him, or thought they had, and now they were out there, prowling until they found him.

I had to get there first. The car seemed to be patrolling round my school, so that's the way I went, pounding down the short cut and through the lane that leads to the playing fields. As I squelched up the muddy track I heard an engine in the main road behind me. When I got to the school field, there was that grey car, parked in the playground. The woman with dark hair – Dr Sheridan – was getting out.

She picked up her mobile phone to speak to somebody, then she trailed round the grounds keeping close to the hedges, searching and calling. I couldn't very well do the same thing, could I? If Wimmer came running out to meet me, we'd both be caught, but I so much wanted him to be with me, to be warm and safe. Then I saw a simply brilliant answer. I ran straight up to her.

"Excuse me," I said, "are you looking for someone?"

For a moment she looked as if she wasn't sure whether to trust me. I tried to look dead innocent and helpful.

"I've lost my – er –my dog," she said. "You haven't seen a curly-coated little dog, have you?"

"No, but I'll help you look," I said. "What's his name?"

She looked as if I'd asked the population of Russia. "Just call 'heel'," she said. "That's what he likes. If you find him, don't get too close. He's very shy, and he bites."

And you don't want me to see that he's got feathers, bat ears, and nocturnal eyes, I thought. I felt a wally, hunting about and shouting "heel", but at least, this way, I could look for him without her wondering what I was up to. If I found him, I'd grab him and run.

No luck. I disturbed a wet hedgehog and a frog, but there was no Wimmer. The rain kept falling, but not so hard. Then my teacher, Mrs Carmody, came out to her car and asked what we were doing.

"I'm looking for my dog," said Dr Sheridan coldly. "He ran away."

"Well, I'm sure he isn't here," said Mrs Carmody.

"I'd better have a look," replied Dr Sheridan. "I think I saw him fl... I mean, er... follow this direction."

"And I'm helping, m-m-miss," I said. I was so cold I could hardly speak.

"Well, I haven't seen it, and the gates will be locked soon when the Head goes home," said Mrs Carmody, firmly. "But the caretaker and I will keep an eye open for your dog."

"I'd better look in the school," said Dr Sheridan briskly, and tried to walk in, but Mrs Carmody put herself in the doorway.

"I'm sorry, I can't allow that," she said. "I promise you, I'll make sure the caretaker looks out for him, but I know he isn't in there. No dog could get into the school without being noticed."

She turned to me. "Jacob, you're drenched. Go home."

"B-b-but miss..."

"Now, Jacob, when you're told," she said, then she added, "but first, get your shoe bag from the classroom. You left your trainers, didn't you?"

No way did I want to go inside. Not when Wimmer was out there. "Sorry, miss, I forgot," I said. "Can't I just leave them tonight? It's games tomorrow, and I'll need them again."

"Yes, and it was football practice at lunchtime, wasn't it, and you came in with those trainers covered in mud and wet grass. Your bag's soaking. I've just seen it. Take those trainers home and get them dried. And get yourself dry, too. You'll catch your death of cold."

I tried hard to think of a way of getting round her. There wasn't one. "Yes, miss," I mumbled, and trudged into the classroom. I still had to find Wimmer somehow. It hurt, not knowing where he was, and if he was safe. I unhooked the shoe bag from my peg. I wanted to hate all of them, and my shoe bag too.

I supposed it seemed heavy because I was cold, wet and miserable. But not that heavy, surely? And it was very, very wet.

I looked inside it. And I'd never felt such a great big smile of happiness inside me as when I looked in that shoe bag and saw Wimmer, fast asleep, curled around my trainers.

I'd been right about being able to find my scent. All I had to do now was to get him home and that shouldn't be too difficult. But Dr Sheridan had parked her car at the gates and I'd have to walk past them. She was in there, talking into her mobile phone and looking from side to side. And she looked as if she'd be there forever. If Wimmer stuck his head out, that was that.

My wet clothes were sticking to me, and I couldn't stop shivering. I was starving, too, and suddenly I realized how late it was. I'd only said I was going to look for a lost ball. Mum and Dad would be frantic with worry, and I honestly hadn't meant to do that to them.

I wished I could have told them about Wimmer from the beginning. I'd have to tell them now. I couldn't keep him a secret any longer.

I didn't dare go home by the main road. The only safe way was down the short cut, across country and through Mrs Bryant's garden again. I felt as if every single step would be too much. I set off over the fence at the back of the school, telling myself all the way – I've only got to get as far as that corner... that tree... that bush... with the bag of wet shoes and wet Wimmer growing heavier all the time.

"It's all right, Wimmer," I whispered. "I've got you. It's going to be all right."

Polly

8

WIM–R

If I'd ever had any doubts about whether it was right to hide Wimmer, I lost them in that cupboard in Newstock, reading through that file. The first page said:

WINGED INTELLIGENT MAMMAL (WIM)
The genetically engineered perfect family pet
Aim
The aim is to produce a pet that every family will want. I estimate that parents will be willing to spend between two and four hundred pounds for an easy-care pet and the demand will be enormous, helping us to keep the price high. If we can create a perfect living toy, we will have a product worth millions within three years.

```
Specifications
```
It must be:

(a) obedient, friendly, and good with children;

(b) clean, self-grooming and easy to care for; must not cause any allergic reaction, (particularly asthma);

(c) able to live on any diet, including leftovers;

(d) easy to exercise;

(e) intelligent, but not enough to challenge the owners;

(f) entertaining;

(g) attractive and endearing – large eyes preferred, and a small tail, which can wag without knocking things over; only mildly affectionate – perhaps it should only *seem* to be affectionate. It must not mind if the owners lose interest in it, so the WIM must not become attached to any one person;

(i) able to enter deep sleep, similar to hibernation, when the owners wish to leave it for long periods.

```
Lifespan
```
Lifespan should be about twelve years, so that a WIM bought for children will be due to die when they grow out of it.

The WIM should be friendly and welcoming, but should not need, nor give, love. Children and young people may like the idea of pets, but they cannot be expected to love them – they become tired of them once the novelty has worn off. A loving pet can therefore become a nuisance, and should not be encouraged.

Dr Harper

There was a hand-written note from Dr Sheridan to Dr Harper. It said:

Keep all WIM files on your personal computer, not at work. At this stage we must work in secret, because of:

(a) our rivals, and

(b) public opinion, which needs to change. This programme is extremely valuable and there is a very real danger that a rival may copy it and produce an animal before we do. Obviously, the first person to register a WIM will own the right to produce more animals. That must be us. Otherwise, all our development money will have been wasted.

Denise

I turned the pages. There were pictures of the weirdest looking creatures, dogs with beaks and cats with doggy coats. There were comments under each one, like, 'not clean enough', 'too noisy', and 'ugly'. Then there was always the one word, 'terminated'.

I turned the page again. Wimmer's picture looked out at me from those appealing big eyes. The number from his collar was underneath, and a few comments.

ASD 15698433 B

The best WIM yet, but too clever, and much too affectionate. Had to be punished to break bad habits – particularly loving behaviour. Must be terminated.

DS

So that was it. A perfect, problem-free pet. A living, cuddly toy, for families who couldn't be bothered to look after anything. Love not needed.

From somewhere along the corridor there was a click, then the sound of a door gliding shut. I heard voices – one of them might have been Dr Harper's – and someone said, 'Goodnight, Lisa!'

It was five o'clock, they were locking up, and if Dr Harper came back and found me in that cupboard I'd be so near dead you couldn't tell the difference. But it was too late. The footsteps came nearer, and I heard his voice.

"I don't want my office cleaned tonight," he said. "I've a call to make."

You just would, wouldn't you, I thought bitterly. I turned burning hot, then cold. There was no time to get out. The only thing to do was to stay in the cleaning cupboard. I held the door closed and hoped he didn't try to lock it. If he did, could I burst out and run for it? I wasn't sure. I put out the light, just in time before he came in.

It was too late to wish I'd never come here. Too late to wish I was at home, doing my homework or playing with Jacob and Wimmer in the garden. Too late to wonder if Mum and Dad were getting worried yet.

There was a clunk as Dr Harper dropped

his briefcase on the floor. I heard a phone bleep.

"Hello, Denise?" he said. "Sorry, my secretary tells me young Katie has gone home. She couldn't stay any longer. As it is, I don't think she had any real information to give us."

Safe so far. He didn't want to admit to her that he'd left me alone, and now he didn't know where I was.

"No, I'm sure the girl didn't know much," he said. "She looked a bit thick to me."

Cheek!

"What about you, Denise? Have you found it? Oh. Pity. Well, are you absolutely sure it was the WIM?"

He listened for a while. I could hear Dr Sheridan's voice twanging away at the other end, but even if I tried to breathe quietly I couldn't catch what she was saying.

Then, at last, he said, "Do you know, Denise, I think you could call it a day. It might not have been the WIM that you saw. In any case, it's probably gone and hidden itself in a wood somewhere, and there's no point in hunting any more."

There was a bit more twanging. She didn't sound pleased.

"Look at it like this, Denise," he said. "We don't actually want to keep the thing. It will die on its own very quickly. It's just another 'R' standard WIM, a reject. We'd done all the observations we needed, and it was going to be destroyed, the day it escaped. I just wish I'd killed it first thing in the morning. It was the best WIM yet, but it had too much parrot in it, and probably too much dog."

So 'WIM-R' meant he was a reject. Well, I hadn't rejected him, and neither had Jacob, and we never would. Dr Sheridan rattled out something else.

"No, Denise, it wasn't that clever," said Dr Harper. "I know it was clever enough to escape, but it couldn't keep itself safe. Too trusting. Too affectionate. Something will have killed it."

She yattered on a bit more. I couldn't hear what she said, but I was starting to hate her.

"Don't be stupid," he snapped. "You know I didn't make it like that on purpose. We couldn't change it. I tried everything. I shouted at it, I starved it. I even gave it electric shock treatment. Nothing worked."

I found I was clenching my teeth. I gripped the door handle tightly. I wanted to run in there and empty his coffee machine over his head.

He laughed. "Yes, it stopped liking me, but its nature didn't change. It wanted to be loved by someone, so it was useless. The what, Denise? Oh, that cat-like animal we made, and the poodle-parrot that we crossed with a monkey. I've destroyed those. And those chihuahua birds all died within days. They were too delicate to live, their skulls were weak."

I couldn't believe this. I hoped she'd stop talking and they'd just go. If I heard any more,

I might be sick. She said something else.

"Yes, Denise, of course we're in big trouble if anybody sees it," said Dr Harper. "But if anyone *had* seen it, it would have been in all the newspapers by now! We'll keep looking out for it, but I'm sure it'll be dead soon. Goodnight, Denise."

I let out a slow, silent breath of relief. Too soon. That wretched woman went on quacking.

"Yes, I copied all his photographs for you," said Dr Harper. "I'll get them for you – they're in the cupboard."

No! No, they mustn't be, I thought, if you can think a scream. I gripped that door handle with my eyes shut tight.

"Just a moment," he said, "they may be in my briefcase."

I heard him walk away. *Click, click* went the locks on the briefcase.

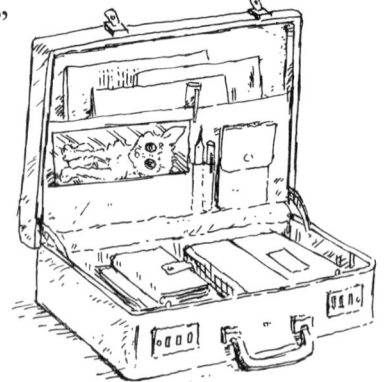

"Yes, they're here. I'll put them on your desk. Goodnight, Denise."

At last! I heard him leave. When I'd counted to twenty I reckoned it would be safe to open the door.

I peeped out. He was gone, and the door to the secretary's office was open, so I made a dash for it, but the next door – the one out of the secretary's room – was locked. I tapped in the numbers from the security code I'd used on the cupboard.

It didn't work. I tried every combination of the four numbers, struggling to stop my fingers shaking. Nothing worked.

I tapped on the door, hoping there might be a cleaner about, but nobody heard. I raked through all the desk drawers again, breaking into a sweat with panic, but there wasn't anything that could be a code.

There was a telephone on the desk. Perhaps I could phone reception and ask them to get me out, or ring home. I picked up the receiver.

Nothing. The lines must have been shut

down. If there was a way of getting through, I didn't know what it was.

It was a nightmare. I kicked and banged at that door, but I knew it was useless and I ended up crumpled up on the carpet with my head on my knees. Then, when everything seemed hopeless, something slotted into my mind.

I saw a picture, very clearly, of Wimmer's face. Below it was that series of letters and numbers. I could see it as clearly as if I had it written in front of me.

ASD 15698433 B

The number on his collar. I'd looked at it and thought about it so much, it was printed in my memory.

It might just be the right one. If they used security codes, they'd change them now and again. What if they used the number of the latest experimental animal?

I tapped it in. When the door opened, it was like escaping into fresh air. The same number got me out of the main door, too, and I ran through the early evening drizzle, not stopping until I was home.

Mum and Dad were on the doorstep, their faces tight and their eyes wide with worry. And there was Jacob, soaked, squelching across the garden, clutching his shoe bag in his arms.

Jacob

9

"What's that?"

Wimmer was in my shoe bag, and that was all that mattered.

I was too cold and wet to speak, staggering across the garden. Mum and Dad were out on the doorstep as if they were starting a search party, and Polly was running down the street looking terrifed.

I wanted to say sorry, but I couldn't get any words out. I tried but I just sneezed, and woke Wimmer. I could feel him wriggling in the bag. Polly pulled mc into the house.

"I'm sorry," I managed at last.

"We can explain," said Polly, "it's important."

"I should think so!" screeched Mum. "Your Dad's just been driving round the streets in the car, looking for you! Barry, go and phone the police and tell them to stop looking. And ring Polly's school, tell them she's here."

Dad escaped to the phone. Mum was pink. I could almost see fire coming down her nostrils. "Get those wet things off, and your shoes, you'll catch pneumonia. We've been worried sick, where have you been? Are you all right? I didn't know where you were, if you were safe..." Then she hugged me.

They do that, mothers. Being hugged when you're wet feels pretty unpleasant, but it means they're glad to see you.

Wimmer loved it. He loved it so much, he put his front paws over the top of the shoe bag. Mum fell over backwards and landed on the stairs.

"What's that?!" she shrieked. Dad, coming down the hall at that moment, stopped dead.

It was too late to do anything. Two pointy ears were on their way up, then his head. He put his head on one side, licked me, and looked at Mum. I could feel his tail wagging.

"It's alive!" said Dad.

Ten out of ten, I thought. Mum was staring at Wimmer. Then she held out her hands.

"Poor little thing!" she said. "It's shivering!"

I tried to explain, but I was chased upstairs

to dry myself and get changed. When I came down, Mum was sitting by the fire cuddling Wimmer and feeding him mashed biscuits. Dad was watching from a safe distance with a puzzled look on his face.

You just can't tell, with parents. I was ready for the ear-bending of a lifetime, I thought I'd be grounded for the next two years. But they didn't say anything, they just looked as worried about Wimmer as I'd been.

Polly was already telling them about finding him and bringing him home, and why we'd done it. That wasn't really fair, because it was my story to tell. I took over and told them why I'd had to go after him that evening, and what had happened. Now and again Mum said "where?" and "Newstock?" and "poor little thing". She said that so often that Wimmer wagged his tail and said, "oo iff ing", and that stopped her saying anything.

"Yes, he imitates speech," said Polly. (She'd been quiet for all of four minutes by then.) "I can tell you why, but make sure you're sitting down first."

Then she told us what she'd found out at Newstock – how they'd invented Wimmer, and what they meant to do with him. Normally she goes rattling on like a tap dancer's feet, but she didn't find it easy to talk about this. When she got to the bit about all those animals being destroyed, she kept glancing at me to see how I'd take it.

When she finished, Dad put his arm round her and told her she'd been very stupid and very brave. She burst into tears and said nothing until Mum handed her the tissues. I just picked up Wimmer and held him. Presently he yawned, and fell asleep in my lap with one paw over his nose.

"Don't worry, Dad, he won't give you asthma," said Polly. "He's non-allergenic." Dad stroked Wimmer's head, and I could tell he liked him.

"I wish you'd told us sooner," said Mum.

"What would you have done?" I asked, and she had to admit she didn't know. And when Polly asked what we should do next, Mum said "eat", which sounded brilliant.

She normally insists on all of us sitting round the table together. But this time, she looked at Wimmer asleep and said it was a shame to disturb him, and I should stay put and she'd bring me my tea.

So I sat by the fire and ate as it grew darker outside and the rain rustled against the windows, and Wimmer slept in my lap. It was so quiet, I could hear the soft huffle of his breathing.

I promised then that I'd take care of him, always.

* * *

"I know he's no trouble, but we can't keep him here," said Mum, after tea was cleared away. "I quite agree we have to look after him, but not here. We're too close to Newstock."

"We could exercise him when nobody's about," said Polly. "That's what we've been doing."

"And what happens when people come round?" said Dad.

"We'll keep him out of the way," I said. "He'll be quiet. He's so good."

"He's been made that way," said Polly. "I know he shouldn't have been made in the first place, but he was, and now he's here. Jacob should keep him."

"He has to stay with me," I said desperately. "He knows me."

Mum stood up. "Colin will know what to do," she said. She left the room, and presently

I heard her pick up the phone.

Wimmer licked my hand, and went back to sleep. Even if they separated us, he'd be mine, and I'd find some way to care for him.

Polly

10
The Hardest Thing

Uncle Colin arrived the next day. He's a bit older than Mum and his hair's going grey, but he wears it in a ponytail all the same. When I came home he was in the kitchen with Jacob and Wimmer, and Mum was trying to pretend that they weren't really in her way at all.

Jacob and Wimmer. Seeing the two of them together was like watching a big brother and a little brother, except that brothers fight. Jacob and Wimmer adored each other. But I couldn't see how we could keep them together.

"I knew this sort of genetic engineering

was going on," Uncle Colin was saying, "but I didn't know it had got this far." He gave me his lopsided smile. "Your mum says that Newstock aren't making any fuss about getting him back."

"No posters," I said. "No announcements. Zilch."

"That's understandable," he said, watching Wimmer chase his tail and fall over. "They need to keep it quiet, if they're going to make a perfect pet before anybody else does –and before the government makes this sort of work illegal."

Wimmer stretched his wings and had a little fly across the kitchen. Mum took him off the washing machine, said "no" very firmly and put him back on the floor.

"They don't care about animals," I said. "They care about the money they can make from selling them. Can't you stop them?"

"Not yet," he said. "They need to be watched and monitored, but I can arrange that. We need evidence of what they're doing. I'll need your photocopies, please. They're vital evidence."

Soon after that, he led Jacob and Wimmer to the sitting room. I sat outside on the stairs. I wasn't being nosy. I've told you, I was worried about Jacob.

When they'd sat down, Colin said, "What do we do about Wimmer, Jacob?"

"I want to keep him," said Jacob.

"I know," said Colin, "but this might not be the best place for him. You've seen where I work, haven't you? It's a good place for animals. We could keep Wimmer hidden and happy, and I promise I'd take good care of him for you. Wherever he lives, he'll still be yours."

"He might pine for me," said Jacob.

"That's something we'd have to wait and see."

"He might escape and try to get back."

"I don't think so, Jacob."

There was a short silence, then in a small voice, Jacob said, "I promised I'd always look after him."

"That's good," said Colin. "But this might be the best way to do it. You could come to see him in the holidays. Come to stay, if you like."

"I could bring him presents," said Jacob, and he sounded a bit less miserable. "And send some pocket money to buy the things he needs."

When he said that, I knew he was coming round to the idea. But coming round to it and liking it aren't the same thing.

* * *

We went after school on Friday. Jacob had Wimmer on his knee in the back seat, keeping his head down so nobody could see him.

It felt like a betrayal. Everybody except Wimmer knew what was going on. It was for his own good, but that didn't make it easy.

"That photocopy," said Dad as he was driving, "I've put my own copy in the bank in a sealed envelope. If anybody from Newstock finds out where Wimmer is and tries to get him, we threaten to publish it."

"Do you think they will?" asked Jacob.

"I'm sure they won't," said Dad. "It's just in case."

* * *

Colin was there to meet us when we arrived. Mum, Dad and I wandered around the animal sanctuary and fed the baby hedgehogs with a dropper. Colin showed us the run in the garden where Wimmer could play without being seen. There was mesh over the top, so he couldn't fly away.

"He'll sleep in my bedroom," said Colin. "He's used to human company, so that's what he'll have."

Jacob gave him one of his old sweaters so

Wimmer would have something of his, and he'd brought him a ball and some biscuits. Then Colin took Wimmer indoors so he wouldn't have to watch Jacob go.

In the car, Mum put her hand on Jacob's shoulder, but he shook it off and turned his face to the window. Nobody dared speak to him all the way home.

Jacob

11
The Future

It was the worst night of my life. I knew we'd done what was good for Wimmer, but that didn't take away the raw hurt inside, as if part of me had been ripped out.

I worked it out. Thirty-five days to half-term and I'd see him again. By then, he'd be following Uncle Colin about instead of me. He might have forgotten me.

I don't know what time I went to bed that night, but I woke on Saturday with an idea.

The papers Polly took from the lab said that Wimmer should live for about twelve years. I was eleven. If Wimmer was new, he still had a long time to live. When I left school I could go and work with Uncle Colin, like I'd always wanted to, and I'd be with Wimmer again. And now it was only thirty-four days to half-term.

Saturday wasn't a good day, but it was bearable. I made a calendar to count the days until I could see Wimmer. I went to bed on Saturday night and went out like a light.

I woke up earlier than I was ready to, because of all the noise. The phone was ringing, which doesn't usually happen at seven o'clock on a Sunday morning, and something was hitting against my window. I yawned and rubbed

my face, and had to force my eyes open before I could pull back the curtains — then I opened the window, fast, and pulled Wimmer inside

before anyone could see his wings, and before I could burst open for joy. I held him while he licked and wriggled and put his paws on my shoulders. Mum was talking on the phone, and she was worried.

"Mum," I called over the top of Wimmer's

head, "if that's Uncle Colin, tell him it's all right. Wimmer's here."

At the other end, Colin must have heard.

"Colin says he can't have found his way..." she began. Then she saw Wimmer wriggling in my arms.

* * *

Newstock closed down very soon after that. Nobody seemed to know why. They just suddenly shut up shop, paid off the staff, and put the building up for sale. I heard that they didn't leave a thing behind, not a filing cabinet, not even a sheet of notepaper. Not even a feather.

People think we've got a funny-looking dog. He's learned to keep his wings folded up when he's out, and not to fly where anybody might see him. He knows when to keep his mouth shut, too.

He still sleeps in my room, and he still likes my trainers, which is weird. And, even now that it's all closed down, he won't go near the Newstock place.

Wimmer likes proving people wrong. The Newstock scientists wanted to make him so he couldn't love anyone, but he does. Even Uncle Colin said he couldn't find his way home. But he did. And they all said he wouldn't be able to live with me.

But he does.

About the author

This book began on a school holiday morning when I was half asleep during the early morning radio news. There was a report about cross-bred animals, and I drifted into a dream about a strange creature made up of different species.

When I woke up I had the idea for this book, and couldn't think why nobody had written it before. I discussed it with a simply brilliant class at Lady Lumley's School in Pickering, so *Wimmer* is for them.